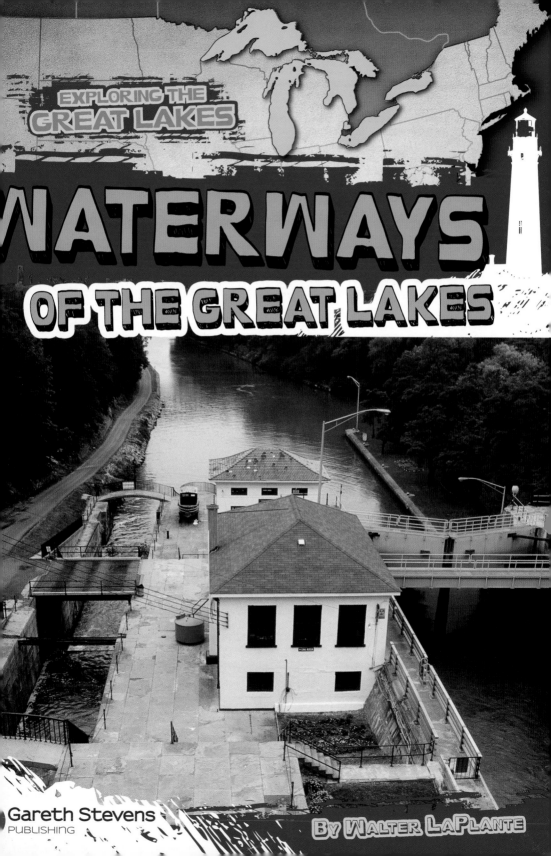

EXPLORING THE GREAT LAKES

WATERWAYS
OF THE GREAT LAKES

Gareth Stevens
PUBLISHING

By Walter LaPlante

Please visit our website, www.garethstevens.com. For a free color catalog of all our high-quality books, call toll free 1-800-542-2595 or fax 1-877-542-2596.

Library of Congress Cataloging-in-Publication Data

LaPlante, Walter.
Waterways of the Great Lakes / by Walter LaPlante.
p. cm. — (Exploring the Great Lakes)
Includes index.
ISBN 978-1-4824-1212-3 (pbk.)
ISBN 978-1-4824-1195-9 (6-pack)
ISBN 978-1-4824-1441-7 (library binding)
1. Great Lakes Region (North America) — Juvenile literature. 2. Saint Lawrence River — Juvenile literature. 3. Waterways — Juvenile literature. I. Title.
F551.L37 2015
917.704—d23

First Edition

Published in 2015 by
Gareth Stevens Publishing
111 East 14th Street, Suite 349
New York, NY 10003

Copyright © 2015 Gareth Stevens Publishing

Designer: Michael J. Flynn
Editor: Kristen Rajczak

Photo credits: Cover, p. 1 Rudi Von Briel/Stockbyte/Getty Images; pp. 5, 14 Map Resources/Shutterstock.com; p. 7 alexvirid/Shutterstock.com; pp. 8-9 Dudarev Mikhail/Shutterstock.com; p. 9 courtesy of the International Joint Commission; p. 10 Russell Marini/Shutterstock.com; p. 11 Ivan Cholakov/Shutterstock.com; pp. 12-13 Alan Copson/Photographer's Choice RF/Getty Images; p. 15 Koekeloer/Shutterstock.com; p. 16 courtesy of the Library of Congress; p. 17 The Evening News/AP Images; pp. 18-19 Songquan Deng/Shutterstock.com; p. 19 http://commons.wikimedia.org/wiki/File:Adam_Beck_Complex.jpg; p. 21 (map) Rainer Lesniewski/Shutterstock.com; p. 21 (Georgian Bay) Jordan Tan/Shutterstock.com; p. 22 Bloomberg/Getty Images; p. 23 Rolf Hicker/All Canada Photos/Getty Images; p. 24 J. L. Levy/Shutterstock.com; p. 25 erandamx/Shutterstock.com; p. 26 Lisa Stokes/Flickr Open/Getty Images; p. 27 Robert Ginn/Photolibrary/Getty Images; p. 29 Ken Ilio/Flickr/Getty Images.

Printed in the United States of America

CPSIA compliance information: Batch #CS15GS: For further information contact Gareth Stevens, New York, New York at 1-800-542-2595.

CONTENTS

Words in the glossary appear in **bold** type
the first time they are used in the text.

THE LAKES AND MORE

Together, Lake Huron, Lake Ontario, Lake Michigan, Lake Erie, and Lake Superior are called the Great Lakes. They're found in east-central North America and are the largest surface of freshwater in the world at 95,000 square miles (246,049 sq km).

The Great Lakes serve as a natural part of the border between Canada and the United States. Eight US states touch the lakes, including Minnesota, Wisconsin, Michigan, Illinois, Indiana, Ohio, Pennsylvania, and New York, as does the Canadian **province** of Ontario.

While the Great Lakes are a key resource, there are many other important waterways in the region as well.

This map shows the individual watershed of each lake. Since they're all connected within the Great Lakes basin, the health of one lake and its watershed affects the **ecosystem** of the whole basin.

BASINS, WATERSHEDS

The terms "watershed" and "basin" are sometimes used interchangeably. They're both areas of land that drain into a body of water. A watershed can be as small as a stream or as large as all the rivers emptying into Chesapeake Bay. A basin is a large area of land shaped like a bowl, with sides slightly higher than the bottom. Each of the Great Lakes has an individual watershed, but together they're called the Great Lakes watershed or the Great Lakes basin.

CANADA

ON

QC

Lake Superior

MI

Lake Michigan

Lake Huron

WI

Lake Ontario

MI

NY

Lake Erie

PA

NJ

IL

IN

OH

MD

DE

UNITED STATES

WV

VA

KY

The Great Lakes are often discussed together, but each lake has its own features. Use this chart to learn more about each of the Great Lakes.

Great Lakes Facts

	LAKE ERIE	LAKE HURON	LAKE MICHIGAN	LAKE ONTARIO	LAKE SUPERIOR
volume					
	119 cubic miles (496 cu km)	850 cubic miles (3,543 cu km)	1,180 cubic miles (4,918 cu km)	395 cubic miles (1,646 cu km)	2,900 cubic miles (12,088 cu km)
average depth					
	62 feet (19 m)	195 feet (59 m)	279 feet (85 m)	283 feet (86 m)	483 feet (147 m)
deepest point					
	210 feet (64 m)	750 feet (229 m)	925 feet (282 m)	802 feet (244 m)	1,332 feet (406 m)
shoreline length					
	871 miles (1,402 km)	3,827 miles (6,159 km)	1,638 miles (2,636 km)	712 miles (1,146 km)	2,726 miles (4,387 km)
states/province					
	Ohio Pennsylvania New York Ontario Michigan	Michigan Ontario	Wisconsin Illinois Indiana Michigan	New York Ontario	Wisconsin Minnesota Ontario Michigan

GREAT HABITATS

The Great Lakes region is huge, and about 35 million people live in it. They're not the only living things, however! Thousands of kinds of plants and animals make their homes in and around the Great Lakes. Fish, including Pacific salmon and walleye, swim in the lakes and waterways. Waterfowl such as Canada geese nest along the shores. Sand dunes, hardwood forests, and coastal marshes are just a few of the **habitats** found in the Great Lakes basin.

The health of Great Lakes' wetlands depends greatly on the health of the lakes. Pollution is just one of the ways the lakes and their habitats can be harmed.

A GREAT RESOURCE

Do you live in the Great Lakes region? You may drink from the Great Lakes! They contain nearly 20 percent of the freshwater in the world and provide drinking water for about 40 million people in Canada and the United States.

If you don't live near the Great Lakes, it's possible you own a product from a business that uses Great Lakes water. Or perhaps some of your food was grown in the Great Lakes basin. The many waterways of the Great Lakes have been used for transportation and shipping for a long time, too. Something you're using or eating could have traveled the Great Lakes before it got to you!

KEEP IT CLEAN!

Farm runoff, waste from cities and industry, and mining have polluted the Great Lakes in the past. **Conservation** groups and laws such as the Great Lakes Water Quality Agreement of 1972 have had a big impact on both cleaning up these problems and stopping them from happening in the future. Still, some people believe the economic benefits of **urban** growth and industry outweigh the water quality issues they bring about.

President Richard Nixon and Prime Minister Pierre Trudeau signing the 1972 Great Lakes Water Quality Agreement.

About one-third of the land in the Great Lakes basin is used for agriculture, including dairy, grains, corn, and livestock.

LAKE INDUSTRY

Thousands of years before Europeans settled in the Great Lakes region, Native American tribes used the lakes and their waterways to move people and goods. When Europeans began exploring deeper into North America through the St. Lawrence River, many chose to settle near the Great Lakes because of the shipping and transportation opportunities.

Today, shipping using the waterways of the Great Lakes is important to the economy of both the United States and Canada. It creates about $35 billion in profits each year and employs almost 230,000 people. In all, about 180 million tons (163 million mt) of cargo travel through the Great Lakes every year.

CATCHING A BIG ONE

Commercial fishing became a big industry in the Great Lakes basin beginning in the 1820s. However, poor management of the lakes led to pollution, habitat destruction, and overfishing. The population of many profitable fish has decreased, and commercial fishing opportunities with them. Laurie Sommers, an author who wrote a book on the subject, said in 2013 that "a few commercial fishermen still make a good living, but Great Lakes ecosystems are in crisis."

The Detroit River was a gathering place for trade before European settlers arrived in the area during the 1600s. Today, Detroit remains a busy port in the Great Lakes region.

THE MIGHTY ST. LAWRENCE

The St. Lawrence River is about 800 miles (1,290 km) long, all of which is found in the Canadian provinces of Ontario and Québec. It has three sections: the freshwater river that reaches from Lake Ontario to near the city of Québec, the St. Lawrence **estuary**, and the Gulf of St. Lawrence that opens into the Atlantic Ocean.

A HISTORIC DISCOVERY

The discovery of the St. Lawrence River was European explorers' first step toward finding the Great Lakes. It was one of the first entryways into the middle of North America they found. French explorer Jacques Cartier first sailed the river in 1534 and returned the following year to follow it farther inland. His discovery led to the French claiming much of the St. Lawrence River valley and lands around the Great Lakes.

The St. Lawrence River is **geologically** a part of the Great Lakes. The lakes are at progressively lower levels from west to east, draining toward the St. Lawrence, which empties into the ocean. The river's link to the ocean is very important for shipping and travel.

In 2008, the eight Great Lakes states signed the Great Lakes–St. Lawrence River Basin Water Resources Compact. The states agreed to work together to manage and protect the lands and waters of the basin.

GET TO KNOW THE RIVERS

Many rivers and streams flow within the Great Lakes watershed. Some are healthier than others, but all are home to plants and animals, as well as people!

The Ottawa River is the main **tributary** of the St. Lawrence River. It's found in east-central Canada, creating a natural border between Québec and Ontario. Samuel de Champlain of France first explored the Ottawa River in 1613. It was a major route for fur traders and **missionaries** into the Great Lakes region. Canada's capital city of Ottawa is found along the river, as are Pembroke, Ontario, and Hull, Québec.

Atlantic Ocean

CANADA

QC

St. Lawrence River   Québec City

NB

Ottawa River   Ottawa

ME

ON   VT

NH   Atlantic Ocean

Lake Ontario   NY   MA

CT RI

Lake Erie   UNITED STATES

NATIVE NAMES

Due to the large number of Native Americans, or First Nations people, who once lived in the Great Lakes region, many rivers and other natural features have Native American names. Champlain named the Ottawa River for one group of Algonquians that lived near it. The Hurons, or Wyandots, lived on the lake now named for them—Lake Huron. Lake Erie is also named for a tribe that lived on its shores—the Erielhonan, or long tails.

The Rideau Canal was built in the 1830s to connect the Ottawa River to Lake Ontario.

The St. Marys River is part of the US-Canadian border, dividing Michigan and Ontario. It flows from Lake Superior into Lake Huron, dropping more than 20 feet (6 m) at one point near Sault Ste. Marie, Ontario. Though the rapids created by the river's sudden drop prevent travel of the length of the river, the Soo Canals and **Locks** bypass them.

The US Environmental Protection Agency (EPA) considers the St. Marys River an "area of concern" due to a history of pollution. However, it has spent years cleaning up places of past pollution and had success. So, there's hope for the future health of the river.

AREAS OF CONCERN

The lasting industrial pollution along the St. Marys River is just one area of concern in the Great Lakes region. The Cuyahoga River in Ohio, Menominee River in Wisconsin, and Saginaw River and Bay in Michigan are a few more. According to the US-Canada Great Lakes Water Quality Agreement, areas of concern are those that "fail to meet the general or specific objectives of the agreement," meaning there has been **environmental** harm there.

The two active locks of the Soo Locks are called the MacArthur and the Poe.

Another part of the natural border between the United States and Canada, the Niagara River divides New York and Ontario. Four of the five Great Lakes ultimately drain into the Niagara, which connects Lake Erie and Lake Ontario.

The Niagara River ends in one of the great natural wonders of the world—Niagara Falls. The falls have two major parts. The Horseshoe Falls on the Canadian side of the border are the larger of the two at about 2,200 feet (671 m) across and 185 feet (56 m) high. The American Falls are about 1,060 feet (323 m) across and 190 feet (58 m) high.

WATERPOWER!

About 20 billion gallons (76 billion l) of Great Lakes water is used to create energy at hydroelectric power plants every day. The Niagara River is one of the top sources of waterpower in North America. The Niagara Power Project has two power plants that use Niagara Falls to create electricity for both Canadian and US households. One is found near Lewiston, New York, and the other is at Queenston, Ontario.

Niagara Falls can be enjoyed from both the United States and Canada.

Three bodies of water connect Lake Huron and Lake Erie in Michigan. The St. Clair River flows from Lake Huron into Lake St. Clair. The Detroit River joins it to Lake Erie. Detroit, Michigan, is found on the Detroit River, as is Windsor, Ontario.

Lake St. Clair is sometimes called the sixth Great Lake. It's much smaller than the other lakes, however, with a water surface area of only 430 square miles (1,114 sq km). That's about 1 percent of Lake Superior! The lake has an average depth of only 10 feet (3 m) and a maximum depth of 21 feet (6.4 m).

YET ANOTHER GREAT LAKE?

Georgian Bay, found on the northeastern end of Lake Huron, is so large that it, too, has been called the sixth Great Lake! It's 120 miles (193 km) long and 50 miles (80 km) wide, with an average depth between 100 and 300 feet (30 and 91 m). There are thousands of islands in Georgian Bay, including the largest freshwater island in the world, Manitoulin Island.

LAKE UPERIOR

MICHIGAN

LAKE MICHIGAN

Georgian Bay

CANADA

LAKE HURON

MICHIGAN

US-Canadian border

ONTARIO

LAKE ONTARIO

St. Clair River

Lake St. Clair

Detroit ○
Detroit River → ○ Windsor

LAKE ERIE

NEW YORK

PENNSYLVANIA

INDIANA   OHIO   UNITED STATES

Until about a decade ago, environmental problems around Lake St. Clair went untreated. Though water pollution, **invasive species**, and habitat destruction have finally been addressed in recent years, both Lake St. Clair and the St. Clair River remain in need of conservation efforts.

Georgian Bay

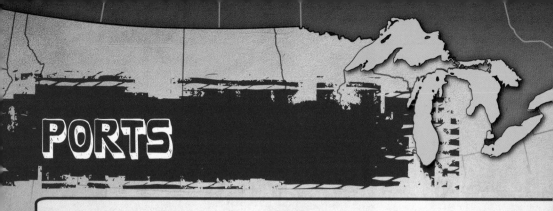

PORTS

As the Great Lakes waterways have been used for shipping and transportation for so long, cities have grown up around the many ports needed for these activities. Today, the largest port in the Great Lakes is also the westernmost point of the lakes: the Port of Duluth-Superior. Each year, about 1,000 ships visit the port, which is part of Duluth, one of the largest cities in Minnesota.

Port of Duluth-Superior

LIGHTING THE WAY

The Split Rock Lighthouse on Lake Superior is one of the many lighthouses in the Great Lakes region. Found between Duluth and Two Harbors, Minnesota, the light was built to help guide ships after shipwrecks occurred in 1905 on the northern shore of Lake Superior. Visitors who climb the lighthouse get a special view of the lake from the top of the 54-foot (16.5 m) lighthouse, which was built on top of a 130-foot (40 m) cliff!

The Port of Thunder Bay in Ontario is also on Lake Superior. The port is one of the most important in Canada. It's a busy hub that handles about 400 ships each year as well as shipping by truck and rail.

The port of Thunder Bay is right by the Ontario city of the same name.

Since the early 1800s, people living around the Great Lakes have been finding ways to improve the region's waterways for shipping and travel. The Erie Canal was completed in 1825, linking the Great Lakes to the Hudson River. This allowed businesses and farmers in the Great Lakes region to ship to New York City and the East Coast without moving their goods through Canada, which was still part of Great Britain at the time.

The Welland Canal first opened in 1829 in southern Ontario. The canal has eight locks and was built to connect Lake Erie and Lake Ontario, bypassing Niagara Falls in the Niagara River.

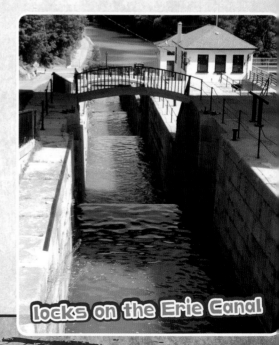

locks on the Erie Canal

CHICAGO SANITARY AND SHIP CANAL

In the late 1800s, **sewage** from Chicago was beginning to cause problems in Lake Michigan. So, a canal was built to change the water flow of the Chicago River away from the lake. The canal has been in the news recently. The Asian carp, an invasive species, may be moving into the Great Lakes through the canal. Measures have been taken to keep it out.

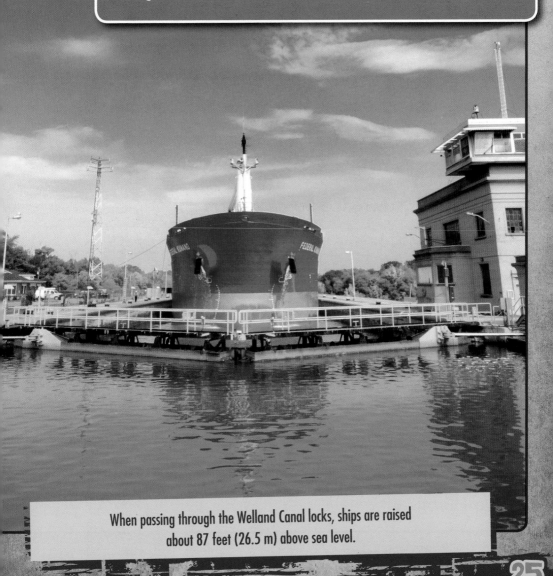

When passing through the Welland Canal locks, ships are raised about 87 feet (26.5 m) above sea level.

Altogether, the many **navigable** waterways of the Great Lakes region are often called the St. Lawrence Seaway. However, there's an official seaway that was completed in 1959.

The St. Lawrence Seaway was undertaken by the US and Canadian governments in order to complete the route from the Great Lakes to the Atlantic Ocean. To do this, two canals, five locks, and three dams had to be built on the Canadian side. Two locks, a 10-mile (16 km) canal, and two dams were built by the United States. In addition, some waterways needed to be dug deeper, including the Straits of Mackinac between Lake Michigan and Lake Huron.

THE SOO LOCKS

The United States's first set of locks on the St. Marys River near Sault Ste. Marie, Michigan, was built in 1855. A single lock had been built in 1797 on the Canadian side, but it was destroyed during the War of 1812. Today, the Soo Locks are the largest waterway traffic system on Earth! Thousands of boats pass through the locks each year, from small passenger boats to "lakers" 1,000 feet (305 m) long.

During the 5-year-long construction of the final seaway connections, about 6,500 people had to move! Roads, bridges, and tunnels were built. Some previously built man-made waterways got updated to accommodate big vessels, like this one.

THE PEOPLE PROBLEM

Many cities have grown around the Great Lakes region since placement on the waterways has always benefited those who live along them. Two of the biggest cities in North America are on the Great Lakes: Chicago, Illinois, and Toronto, Ontario. However, these cities and many others tend to grow in all directions, or sprawl. This destroys habitats and creates pollution.

While economic growth is good for everyone living around the Great Lakes, continued conservation efforts are needed. You can help! Many cities have cleanups of nearby waterways that you can join in. Writing to your local representatives about environmental issues is another way to contribute to lake conservation, too.

TOURISM

Tourism is big business in the Great Lakes region. From Niagara Falls to the 19th-century theme park on Mackinac Island, there are many places to visit on the beautiful waterways. As economically important as tourists are, the more people who visit a place, the dirtier it's bound to be! If you visit a Great Lakes beach, park, or sail the waterways, make sure you pick up your trash and don't leave anything behind.

The beauty of the Great Lakes region can only be preserved if people work to keep it clean.

GLOSSARY

conservation: the care of the natural world

ecosystem: all the living things in an area

environmental: having to do with the natural world in which a plant or animal lives

estuary: an area where the ocean's tide meets a river

geologically: having to do with the history of how Earth formed

habitat: the natural place where an animal or plant lives

invasive species: one kind of living thing likely to spread and be harmful when placed in a new area

lock: a closed area in a canal used to raise or lower boats as they pass from one water level to another

missionary: someone who travels to a new place to spread their faith

navigable: deep enough and wide enough to allow ships to pass through

province: a political unit of a country

sewage: waste matter from buildings

tourism: the business dealing with those who travel to visit a place

tributary: a stream or river flowing into a larger body of water

urban: having to do with the city

FOR MORE INFORMATION

BOOKS

Bekkering, Annalise. *Great Lakes*. New York, NY: AV2 by Weigl, 2013.

Peppas, Lynn. *The St. Lawrence: River Route to the Great Lakes*. New York, NY: Crabtree Publishing Company, 2010.

Thompson, Linda. *Building the Erie Canal*. Vero Beach, FL: Rourke Educational Media, 2014.

WEBSITES

The Great Lakes
www.enwin.com/kids/water/the_great_lakes.cfm
Learn more about the Great Lakes on this website just for kids.

Great Lakes Children's Museum
www.greatlakeskids.org
Found in Traverse City, Michigan, the Great Lakes Children's Museum offers lots of fun programs and events to learn about the Great Lakes region.

INDEX